Seasons
of the Self

MAX COOTS

Seasons
of the Self

Skinner House Books

SEASONS OF THE SELF

Published by Skinner House Books,
an imprint of the Unitarian Universalist Association,
25 Beacon Street, Boston, MA 02108-2800.

ISBN 1-55896-285-9

DEDICATED TO MY BROTHER,TERENCE

THIS YEAR

A year's a year!
A string of kindergarten beads strung once-upon-a-time:
  Of flighty minutes for clocks to tsk-tsk about,
  And days in simple black-and-white conformity.
For clocks and calendars it's so.
My time is something else again:
  Minutes sometimes hours long,
  And days of seconds or eternities.
On calendars the seasons march in pat procession across neat-numbered
  months.
For me, and others of my ilk, the seasons are not just holidays of green
  or white.
I sometimes sense some stronger seasons in myself,

9

Where time is rearranged as something clocks could never tell:
A time in some subjective order all its own
Where Winter sometimes starts in June and leaves grow gold in Spring;
When light is long or short in spite of sun,
And Winter comes when grass is green except in me.

The village clock keeps time as time should be,
But I blaspheme Old Chronos with months I make and seasons centered
  in myself.
My year:
    A year that is my life—
    A life that is my time—
    My time that ought to be eternity enough.

TOWERS OF THE PAST

If I were twice as old as I am now, I could tell you how it was when I
    was just a boy,
And you would smile indulgently and maybe even listen, for old men are
    supposed to rummage through what's been.
There is something pleasant in watching old men pick over the places of
    the past, selecting out forgotten fragments for us to see, as if their days
    were made of old, frail glass.
But at my age you're supposed to live the present in the future tense, full
    of tomorrows and devoid of yesterdays.
It's presumed the young think so little of the past because they have so
    little past to think about.
But the truth is, life is not that way.
There are no specialists of time.

Even a child owns a yesterday and the old a tomorrow.

We condemn young men to chaos when we forbid them to remember anything that was,

And make old men fools when we presume their pasts are merely playthings of senility.

So, though I'm only half as old as I ought to be, I'll tell you how it was when I was just a boy.

I remember then that there was no measurable time that you could count like notches on a stick.

Time was not told by calendars and clock, or by seasons that came on the 21st of months.

Life was what you did and time was how you felt about what was.

Time was a ragged irregularity.

There were hours that were only minutes:

When there were horse chestnuts to gather, warm and waxy to the touch, under September trees;

When there were fleets of twigs to launch down April gutters

Or tadpoles to catch in new May ponds;

When there were treasure maps to draw, slingshots to try, or Saturday sandwiches to eat on a high hill north of town.

Then there were these things that made seconds into centuries—that made Winter in the midst of Summertime.

The kitchen clock might whisper away the days and calendars on walls might count out time like playing cards (equal numbers to every player),

But inner clocks kept a different time at oddly differing speeds, depending on outer quality and inner state of mind.

I say this to remind you how child-time was, and, maybe, to hint that our time is still that way: irregular—counting odd-shaped minutes despite what the liars on our wrists may say.

I remember, too, how it was running in and out between the time invented by adults and the lived time of my own self—back and forth as freedom and demand allowed, letting the screen door of indifference slam behind me on my way out.

Both the coming in and going out were good: one for security, the other for growth.

Of all the places I went, one was especially special.

(Remember now, life was what you did and time was how you felt about what was.)

That place was my grandparents' farm.

(This may be so personal as to be irrelevant to anyone but me. Yet, maybe not, if, as I suspect, everyone remembers some past place or person of this sort.)

That place was like another time, even as adults count time.

There I had weeks of a world apart.

Even the tall thin clock on the kitchen shelf told a different time from those in town: they called it "Old Time," and this was truer than they knew.

There were for me there:

Horses to drive at the end of black leather lines that made me both afraid of them and proud of me.

Endless cats, different from year to year, yet all scampering stiff-tailed from nowhere at the sound of milk.

A tall-chimneyed gauze-mantled lamp for the nights and hunts for toads in the dirt-floored cellar filled with potato smell for the days.

A grotesque milk separator turned by a hand that began in fun and ended in an impatient ache.

A gray weathered barn, roofed with crazy-quilt tar paper outside and swallows in, and filled with hay for rainy days.

And most my own, a pasture gully, like a tiny valley, too small for much adult use, but excellent for tow-head "Indians" who lived royally on its chokecherries, and stalked the water bugs and crabs with an aboriginal tin can.

There I had a world apart.

Then there was time that was once.

And then, and it seems suddenly, it didn't matter anymore. I traded games of Indians for games of growing up, and substituted leaves of books for leaves of poplar trees.

Then I became a man.

Now I'm far enough from childhood to have overcome a young man's embarrassment about the child he was.

Now I sometimes pick over pieces of that place and time, and smile, and find them good.

As if to write a postscript to such reminiscenses, this Summer, I was down that way when idiocy or maybe some intimation of mortality made me stop there.

I knew that no one by my name lived there anymore, but someone with an alien name like Jones or Smith instead.

I knew that nothing stays,

That no one goes back again,
That past is past.
But still I wanted to take my children back with that foolish faith of fathers,
  who forget that a child's past is a parent's present.
I said I wanted them to see the place, though if anyone cares for truth,
  I wanted to catch a creek-crab in a baking powder can, just one more
  time.
I didn't though.
The crabs were there, but I was twenty-five years too late to catch the
  best ones.
Besides, I didn't have a baking powder can.

To the eye the pasture gully was about the same as then.
New cows had kept it so, with birch trees up one slope and berry canes
  down the other one.
Wild grape grew where wild grape had grown.
There were even bull thistles in blossom there.
I used to chew their blossoms until I could spit what looked like real tobacco
  juice.
But I left the thistle blossoms where I left the crabs: in another time.
I really had no other choice.
Once it was the place where improbabilities were probable and miracles
  were everyday events.
I remembered that, and that was good enough.
The barn was quite another thing.
Whoever lives there now (in the house, I mean) . . . I can't recall the name
  . . . must have no need of barns.
A barn roof's sag is a graph that tells how much people need the barn,
  and that barn's stock had slipped considerably.
From inside I could see the sky was doing pretty well at patching holes.
Not much tar paper outside or swallows in.
What little hay was left was left for dust to take.
Cows can keep a gully about the same, but it takes people for barns to
  last.

15

Cows do it by being cows. People have to care.
Whoever lives there now must have no need to care for barns.

Out in back, where burdocks had chased the chickens from the yard—at
least there were no chickens there—was the shell of what had once been
a car.
(My grandfather kept his packages of Red Man in the pocket on the door.
I chewed bull thistle myself.)
I wished the burdocks had chased it away before I had come back, or dust
taken it, or, at least, somehow cows had kept it as it was, for more than
any other thing, it touched the time that was once and the time that
was still mine.
I have outgrown gullies and have no need of barns.
But that one thing, forgotten more than all the rest, I had not outgrown.
I wished I had.

Gully, barn, and car: titles of a time; variations on a theme.
The place was Eden once when I was in my genesis. In it grew every good
thing the land knew how to grow: creek-crabs, black-cap berries, wild
grape, and mint.
As I've said, it seems to stay about the same, should any other child find
where it is.
A child would know what to do with it.
If not, I could not tell him, though I remember it.
I could not tell him because I don't live there anymore.
I have grown tall enough and do not need to chew thistle blossoms now.
Chokeberries will not satisfy my hungers anymore.
I say this without regret, though sometimes I think I'd like to meet the
child I was. But then, what could we talk about? We're not very much
alike.

Nobody can claim a time or place forever.
No one owns the land.

The land is an inheritance; a loan used variously: sometimes by apple trees—sometimes by men.

Each does something on or with the land . . . and maybe it does something back worth remembering long afterward.

But each has its coming time and going time, back and forth between the lived times of ourselves and the longer time of earth.

I say this too without regret.

It's only things that have no life that have no death.

Only rocks have immortality on earth.

No one owns the land, but if it matters—if places have significance—it's because someone touches them with mind. A place is really whatever is in you to have it be. The dignity of old worn apple trees, the sudden sense of solitariness in the cry of crows, the strength of rocks, are qualities of mind that neither tree nor bird nor stone possesses.

It's trading in old Edens for new that counts, and knowing how long is long enough to stay.

The barn was quite another thing.

It was not so much a place as a box of things to do.

It contained:

    Empty space to fall through from rafter to mow,

    Searches for a vagrant hen with a secret nest of expectant eggs, or a brood of newborn mice,

    The exhilaration of tightroping on a beam,

    Hay hills to storm in every war that ever was,

    A smorgasbord of smells, as various as life.

We all have had toy boxes.

In time attics get some of them. Neighbor children the rest.

With barns, obviously attics won't do, nor children either.

As no one cares or needs to care in this case, either frost or fire or wind, whichever proves appropriate, will take it down someday.

The earth means to have it back.

I say this with a shrug.

17

I'm through with it.
I have no need of barns.

But out in back, the car—a rusted regret I had not remembered.
It was not some place I had outgrown nor a thing I had left from lack
of need.
Its being there touched people, places, of my past and made if different
from the rest.
It was a focus for faces, a once-was and a still-is thing.
I wished it wasn't and I wished wrong.
I confused a relic with reality, as if the end of it were the end of the people
of my past.
We deceive ourselves with clocks and calendars and dates on graves.
Lived time is never by the numbers.
We deceive ourselves with talk of what was, what is, what will be, though
time is indivisible.
The past is in the present.
Even flesh has its continuity, just as mind has memories.
There is no going back. No need for it, when past is always rushing up,
however changed it seems.
No one need regret the rust. It's as it has to be.
But there is a compensating timelessness in time, not always measurable,
but through it we make maturity and eternity in time.

WINTER

No one says much good of Winter,
Except as something hard that exaggerates the Spring reprieve;
Spring, people seem to understand.
Spring speaks to us when Winter has been so long we seem bone-cold
   and brown-husked in house-bound apathy.
It speaks now green, coming out of mud, like a waking up.
Though Spring is really nothing much compared to Summertime,
Its barely warm feels very warm,
And the bits of color that spot the new-bare ground sparsely
Seem to the mind as though the world were full of crocus heads and green
   spikes pointing up.
How we resent those last streaks of snow that hide in shadows!
Even the mud seems good.

19

Poets and backyard potterers extol the virtues of Spring with words and
   seed-catalog banners.
Even yesterday's snow-happy children celebrate with the launching of a
   thousand twig-ships in March snow turned to April puddles.
No one says much good of Winter.
If anyone had a kind word to say of it, it would be drowned out,
For Spring is full of noise for all its quietness.

For most, "Out of sight, out of mind" is true,
And, as if to make it truer faster, the brooms of Spring cleaning set about
   to sweep it out of doors, rags wash it from the windows, rakes scrape
   it from the lawn,
As if it were a dirty thing.
No one says much good of Winter.

Sometimes, though, house-free people walking out in Spring will stop in
   passing to comment smugly on past temperatures and snowfalls.
They talk like veterans from some victorious army at peacetime conventions,
Recalling how it was when Winter was—
How it was they went, hat-helmeted and coat-armored, making tracks
   through its efforts,
And spotting its white-on-white with wool-colors.
They reminisce about how they went with shovels to chop Winter walls
   into passes and paths.
They speak as though cold and snow would never happen again.
Spring is a cockiness in people, like a bad night dream remembered with
   a laugh at noon.

Then Summer settles in.
Spring-pride grows satisfied by June.
It's a kind of fickleness in July and August that brings complaints about
   the heat.
The Winter veterans, gone from Spring excitement to Summer that brought

too much green to appreciate, call across the lawnmower handles, "Hot enough for you?"

Change again from August dustiness to ripe September.
Indifferent Summer changes then to Fall,
And vagrant thoughts of other snows intrude from time to time,
But only mildly yet, for everything gets excited, as in Spring, with color.
But we, like trees, live out the easy days with a kind of mock bravado—
A sort of last defiant smile for cold nights and falling leaves.

But even Autumn ends,
Frost sees to that.
What cold had turned too-much green to never-enough yellow, red, and
    rust,
Having gingerly felt its first way with bribes of brilliance,
Seems to grow more confident.
One day it melts the late squash blossoms and curls the garden leaves
    from green to brown with nothing happy in between.
If we could we wouldn't talk of it.
But we have to speak of it, because of children.
They think it's snow.
We have to tell them, "No, it's frost!"

Leaf color dries to brown,
Is raked,
Counted as nothing much,
And burned,
Except the few pressed and waxed ones that sentiment keeps on into snow-
    time—
Or the few rebellious ones that the wind hides tangled in among bush
    stems—
Or that summer gardeners heap for compost or for winter coats on plants
    that can't retreat indoors in pots in sunroom windows.

After so much color in our eyes—
After this, we haven't many words to say of Autumn's last few days.
It just is.
No one says so.
It just is.
And we let it go.
A sort of dull, bare waiting after doing.
Autumn tiredness settles on us, who having seen them oftentimes before—
Spring, Summer, Autumn—retire to wait,
While children, not sure just where it is that they belong, go from one
    side of house doors to another,
Indecisively,
Tracking mud from cold October rain inside to remind us of the past.
A dull, bare waiting,
Looking out at stick-trees.
No one says much of it.
It just is.

Then one night or day—
It's all the same one time as another—
The waiting ends.
A white ending.
Sometimes it is in thick tangled blobs that melt on whatever little summer
    sun the ground has stored.
Sometimes it is in sharp, fast pieces hissing.
Sometimes it is a slow, dogged laying down of layer-upon-layer.
But however it comes, it always finds us unprepared.
    Yet wait!

Strange that we should take the leaves as truth,
And think that just because they fall the tree is dead.
A pulling back, a rest, a new anticipation, yes!
But the leaves are liars—
Bright, gaudy things catching our eyes with their clown suits,

Then falling down and mired,
To make us think it is the end.
Leaves are liars!
Snow is just as much beginning as it is end.
As much prologue as epilogue.

The farmer used to know things about the snow we ought to know.
The farmer used to call the snow "the poor man's fertilizer."
A homely sort of name—
A crude, but honest thing to call this drifting promise.
It is next year's water and next year's grain,
Fall's end and Spring's beginning.
So, when was it we learned that the earth would end?
In Autumn?
Never!

When did we ever learn that life was always Summertime and Spring and
  harvest time?
When was it that someone guaranteed a year of twelve Julys, complete
  with everlasting picnics and never-ending potato salads?
What sort of quaint, mistaken almanac said Spring could come without
  December—
That life was all in June—
That May and August go on forever?
Even Winter in ourselves may be the poor soul's fertilizer,
And Spring within can come only if some Winter has come first—
Can come, if something like a seed is kept alive through wintering, to sprout
  and grow.
To sprout and grow because of Winter and the wintering.
Like earth, we have our seasons too.

Now that we think of it, we knew this even then, back when in Summer
  we grew complacent in its sun,
Or when in Fall we reaped the earth, as though all life was caught and
  wrapped and stuffed in a pumpkin shell, to be picked, then lost through
  Winter eating.
We knew better, even then,
But snow makes for forgetting, so it seems.

EASTER

By now I've had enough of Wintertime.
Too much, if my reaction to the weather means a thing.
I start to take the weather personally.
No one ever should, but I admit I do.
By now I get a little April foolish about thermometers and things.

Last week when a day or two was strangely warm, I found four or five
    inch-high bulbs of rhubarb coming up, and jumped at spring-contentment
    ahead of time.
It wasn't worth it when the ground turned white again.
In these past days when drunken flakes teased down, I almost hated them,
    as if the gods were bullies and meant the snow for me alone.
Where weather is concerned I'm such an April Fool.

At least I'm not alone in this.

There's something pagan in the way I feel.

It's almost as if I could believe, as ancient people did, that along in March or April, Winter fought with Summer for the earth, and finally compromised with Spring.

It's like a game with seasons taking sides.

It's all snow and ice and cold, then thaw-water making pools by day that night shapes back to ice, then thaw again.

The premature impertinence of something daring to leave the ground and grow.

Then, quick revenge that comes, as snow, to Winter-wish the change away.

It gets to seem quite personal.

Because it does I'd say I know what it was like, centuries ago, when people and their priests paraded Winter out in ugly idol forms, sang psalms to Spring so it would come, and saw in seasons death and life, and death and life again.

I'm not much different, for all my scientific sophistry.
Not by this time of year, at least.

If I feel this, then I must understand just why it was the old ones, ages
    past, imagined gods who died in Wintertime and rose again in Spring:
Adonis; Attis and Dionysis; Osiris rising with the Nile; Demeter and Virbius;
    Proserpine coming back from underground, and Balder with his colored
    robes like Easter eggs.
It's no chance of fate that these gods were thought to come from catacombs
    this time of year.
It had to be an April kind of thing to make much sense to people tired,
    like me, of Wintertime.

Oh, I can see it all quite clearly now, the why of it.
They didn't understand.
Except with that crude understanding of the human heart that needs warmth
    after cold and green to wipe out Winter white.
I sometimes think theirs is the greater truth:
The understanding, not of science, but of soul.
The seasons and the saviors were so mingled that it's hard to know which
    one came first and brought the other one along.
Spring came first!
The gods and godlings came to mind to make some supernatural sense
    of Spring.
But it didn't matter, even then.
It doesn't really matter now.

But I grow pagan the end of March and start to take the seasons too much
    to heart.
Too much? Maybe not . . .
Maybe we ought to take the seasons personally;
Identify ourselves with ancient, primal hungers of history—
To know that past, though past, is never really dead,
That we are now what we were once, and what it always has meant to
    be alive and human, Winter, Fall, or Spring.

We haven't changed that much.

But we have changed.

We can't expect to put our spirits in ancient shapes, though some will try.

Some venerate an ancient God, attach themselves by strings of beads to him, and grieve a Winter grief because he died.

And then, pretending, make mock surprise that he should rise again, year after year, from the tomb their fancy and their faith had laid him in.

But for all my pagan, earthy inclinations this time of year, I can't quite go so far as to adore Adonis like some ancient Greek, praise Proserpine, or sing old Christian canticles.

I know there's truth in myths, but I know what I know,

And these aren't enough, not even in my April foolishness.

I cannot be content to celebrate some ancient resurrection and think it's done, completed, over with.

Life goes on and on.

Life will not stay content at any time of place or mind.

I would as soon wave cattails as I would palms.

For one is about what once was and was once and only once.

The other says something about what is going to be,

Not about antiquity, but something April-new—

Something about my world and me.

Don't misunderstand me.

I think I said *understood* about Attis and Proserpine.

I dare anyone to have more reverence for ancient reverences than I,

But I need a celebration about my life that speaks the Spring-inspired word about my life and death, about me, as I live and die, through my cycling seasons, days, and years.

Catechisms say but half the truth,

And Spring says something more, more close at hand.

But even Spring is not enough for me!

I have some restless need to understand.

Like the poet, I have to ask: "To what purpose, April, do you return again?"

I am not content with promises of little leaves or crocus sprout.
To smell of April earth is good.
But even that does not quite answer me in my late-Winter–early-Spring
   attempt to understand what I am, and what I am about.

Flatly speaking, I am more than mud and grass!
A man is not a mindless seed that Spring will bring to foliage and fruit
   without a by-your-leave,
Just as he is not a .god.
The Spring-born sense of our divinity must be more deep in us than distant
   saviors or fresh-turned sod.

Both old religious pieties and mindless Spring are good,
But both are little more than spectacles for memorized memorials and earthy
   eagerness,
Unless they're more than idols for a once-a-year idolatry.
If understood as parables and parallels to our own waking up and coming
   back to life—
If transferred from altars and garden plots to our own lives, the worlds
   of Spring that priests preach and robins sing become sensible for us again.
We need Passover and we need Spring;
Easter and a sense of God Incarnate in the least of these: myself and you.
We need to know more than just that old men thought that old gods rose
   again,
And more than that every year some April comes and leaves a flowering
   shrub and warms the rain.
We need the sense of deity to crack our own hard, brown December husks
   and push life out of inner tombs and outer pain.
Unless we move the seasons of the self, and Spring can come for us, the
   Winter will go on and on.
And Easter will remain a myth, and life will never come again,
Despite the fact of Spring.

All Winter and through March the hollyhock stands up where it should
   not be.
A dry stick of a thing.
A mockery of itself.
It might have wanted once to break, be covered up, mired in earth,
But ground-ice found it first,
And it was caught.
Frozen in.

   In March the days seem like so many hollyhocks: iced tight.
Motionless,
Except for what senseless whipping back and forth the wind can give.
It doesn't mean a thing, this moving in the wind.

It's motion without life.
Days seem like that in early March.

   Then motion comes.
We never seem to know just when it comes—
You'd think we would after so much Winter-waiting, but we never do.
By surprise, one day March moves.
It suddenly has a movement more than just a moving in the wind.
Not by the calendar. I do know that,
Because the hollyhock was still caught deep in ice on the 21st of March.
It began behind my back while I was too engrossed with Winter-weariness.
What made it move is quite beyond my knowing.
Maybe it was rain—cold to my face—too cold, but warm enough to shrink
   the snow.
It seemed as though the ground beneath came up and out.
It seemed that way.
Really the snow went down, and ran in rivers in the road to be whispered
   away under the passing wheels to wherever it is that old snow goes.
It's all a mystery to me.
It's quite enough it went.
I'm satisfied!
   A few hummocks of dirty snow still crouch in shadows, under a bush
   on in some corner under cool, dark leaves, like April blasphemies.
But even these must go.
The wind will find them out.

   The snow-melt is like an attic door unlatched to show its insides out;
To show the lawns as catch-alls for forgotten things:
   Brown leaves October rakes had missed,
   Sodden papers spelling out last December 5th, as if the English sparrows
      cared to read our past,
   Broken toys,
   Last Fall's jacket buttons,
   Things like that.
A Spring surprise of dirty things.

House-freed children running out make size-four footprints in the lawns.
They look,
And soon turn archaeologist to gather Autumn sticks like bones of mast-
odons,
And bring the broken soldier and the sodden cotton dog inside as idols
of some ancient ritual.
Children love such discoveries,
But then, their eyes see better than ours do, sometimes.

For us, April rain is not always kind.
We like its washing-out of Winter,
But, even so, it shows so much that should be hid, and was till now.
Caught in broken stems, wedged in around the lilac's base, or scattered
where the grass has not yet grown its green, are so many lost, forgotten,
shabby things.
It makes our lawns look like our lives:
Unkind memories,
Old guilts,
And last year's shames.

But lawns, like lives, need seeing to—
Need cleaning up.
At least in Spring there is the will for it!
So soon we turn to raking up and burning up.
Spring is a courage after Winter-weakness that sends us to cleaning out,
As though the dirt that Winter stored must be chased away like ancient
witches.
Spring is a courage.
It lets the empty stem of hollyhock fall free to look as dead as it had been
when it stood tall in ice in Wintertime.
Spring is a courage that lets the old things die and scatters them across
our eyes—the things that ought to be done and over with.

Spring is not so much a dying time as it is a time that shows what has
  already died.
It's not an easy sight!

There ought to be a season when we have to recognize the living from
  the dead.
Early Spring is such a time.
We needn't look!
We can turn our eyes away, I guess, and let the later grass grow up around
  the time-lost things,
And fool ourselves.
We can,
But come another Spring and there they'll be,
And more besides.
And what if some Summer's grass could not grow high enough some year
  to hide it all?
What then?
No, it's better to have to see it all, each Spring, to somehow rake it up
  and burn it up.

There is a kind of cure in the rake's sound—
A sense of rightness in rake tines clawing up dead grass and sticks and
  things, and leaving as they go neat lines across the lawn.
It smells like youth again to smell the smoke of burning yesterday's debris.
Even rake-born blisters have a good hurt.
I only wish we still threw dusty rugs across a line and drove out the piled-up
  past with curled wire beaters.
The dull explosions of wire-smacked sound against a rug seemed somehow
  clean.
No matter!
There is still cure in getting rid of Wintertime.

Spring is a finishing,
But it is beginning too.

The hollyhock that Winter's whimsy kept upright past its time had been
   provident with seeds,
As if it knew it had to go to earth again.
In Fall its flowers dropped,
But at their base each left a button, rim-filled with seeds like coins,
And now I see them scattered into dirt and wet from melted frost.
Sometime soon a few of them—enough for hollyhock-hungry eyes—will
   sprout.
May and June will see the hollyhock again, as though the past had never
   been.
Spring is a defiant time!

   The earth is full of stubbornness!
I went, as soon as weather said I could, to dig out Summer's last few parsnip
   roots.
Turning them, one by one, out of the ground, I dug into Spring's stubborn-
   ness:
   A weed root with its spot of green already coming out,
   Fat sluggish angleworms,
   A tuber with a sprout.
Mingled with some Autumn leaves the grapevine had held against its base,
   I found the bulbous heads of rhubarb sprouts—
   Almost too red against the ground—
   And some had even started to unfold a crinkled frill of red-green leaf,
   as if eager to become some child's pretend umbrella.
All this, so soon, even before the ground looked more than bare.
So soon, for Spring to green-thumb its nose at Winter, with all this early
   coming out of hiding.
Surprising to smell the soil-smell now, as though it had never been before,
To anticipate the Summer's green in the pale grass and feel the August
   heat in the April sun,
To stand and gawp at the sound the first few robins make!

I like to think I know what Spring is all about,
Just because I've lived it all again, as if I never felt a Spring before.
It makes me think I know so much about Spring things and never-was-before
    things.
I know, of course, that nervous sparrows, tulip tongues, and even mud
    are miracles to make me stammer in my ignorance.

We've come to be so clever and so high-born with all our rituals
That we've forgotten how it was the shapes of gods were made.
We celebrate our Eastertimes and talk of resurrected gods and men in our
    forgetfulness.
It's only right that such ideas should come in Spring.
The sorry thing is that we don't remember how it was the resurrection
    hopes began.
We forgot, and didn't have our priests walk out across the earth and see
    it waking up.
We didn't go ourselves, like children in the mud, to see what things the
    Winter left and what the Spring was sneaking in behind our words.
We didn't stop in April rain to touch the earth—
To crack the hard, dry husk of old theologies, and let the green of life
    reach out.

We ought to rake up the sophistry of sacred silliness,
And simply walk upon the land,
And stop to hear its yawning after sleep,
And see it stretch up for sun.
We ought to join again the family of the earth.
We ought to go as worshipers
And see the face of God speak to the earth
And speak to us
    From out the folds of burdock sprout
    And from the moist, brown mass of April clod.

GO FLY A KITE

For two weeks now, since the weather broke into Spring, calendars to the
    contrary, I've meant to replace the driveway stones the snowplow pushed
    out of bounds along with last December's snow.
But, as yet, I haven't put my good intentions around the handle of a rake.
No excuse for it.
At least not any my ancestors would have taken as good enough.
They used to dote on duties done in proper season—
And Spring has always been the time to clean up what Winter leaves when
    Winter's done.
I have been busy, though neither yard or rake know anything about my
    busyness.

I have felt some few pangs of guilt seeing others so adept at April things,
But mostly I'd rather keep my guilts for something more than grass.

Besides, I know whatever April leaves undone, May will keep for me to do.

Right now the wind is right for kites and me.

To neighbors, who believe, I guess, that there is nothing left of boys when boys grow up, I must look the perfect fool cutting across their lawn to reach the field behind their house, kite, tail, and string . . .

And trailing my own kind of tail of children, who somehow know what wind is for.

I used to need a child along; a boy or two to hide behind, so I could look as though I went to supervise and nothing more.

I used to hope my neighbors would stay indoors, until I got out of sight at least,

But now I've grown up (or down) to caring more for kites than for bemused smiles.

This Spring I've been busy flying kites, and I don't need children to help me get my courage up—just a good wind will do.

I have no disdain for those preoccupied with ground things now.

Spring is the right time for making sense of soil.

It's really a toss-up which is best to be busy with: earth or air.

But, for a while, I'll be intent with celebrating the season on the end of a string, whenever the wind says I can.

No doubt some armchair analyst could find this of interest, suspecting me of trying to go back to the boy I used to be, of wanting to shed responsibilities, and even call my kite string umbilical.

He might be right, though I am less impressed with such reasoning than I once was.

He might be right, but it seems to me there's something good to be said for kites and flying them.

For one thing, I know of no better way of getting away from earth a while; away from tattered papers, scattered sticks, and dog-deserted bones.

All Winter long I had to keep my mind down for fear of ice.
Winter here is a long time to be so constantly concerned with what's underfoot.
I get Winter-weary of so many cold considerations.

Adulthood can't be just drifts and getting through and making paths, without some time off.
There ought to be some time to get away a while, and, for me, up two hundred feet of string is a good way to go.
It sounds like just so much immature escape—or would, if kites weren't what they are.
But kites won't let you go and not come back.
They have a sense of reality in the way they work.
You can only go as high as the wind allows, for one thing;
And for another, only as far as the string will reach.
And if you think to extend it by adding ball on ball of string, eventually the very weight of the string itself makes an end to running out too far . . .
Or else the wind blows up too strong for the strength of the string . . .
Or the wind dies down, too weak to hold it up,
And, somehow, everything comes back to earth, as everything must sometime.
It's as it ought to be.
Everything has limits, and something always sees we know where the limits are.
And that's as it ought to be.
Kites are good that way, and I've broken several being taught.

But for a time, it's good to get away from the earth a while.
Kites have a way of making you look up and out . . .
Too much of looking in and down can be diminishing.
To see too much too close breeds the familiarity that breeds contempt.

We know there has to be some distance between two people to keep a love alive.
Too much self-analysis, like too much looking in a mirror, makes for too little self-respect or world-respect.
There ought to be some time to get away a while.

Not everyone will choose my way, or should.
But I'd suggest that whatever way it is, it have no real purpose beyond itself.
There's enough of good and bad to come back to when you must come back.
There's always something dutiful to do, something yet we must become, someone to be met responsibly, and lawns to rake.
Whatever way your sometimes going takes, make it for its own good sake: conflicting with no one else, abusing no one or his needs, and adding nothing to what you possess except your perspective.

And it ought to be a little bit absurd to everyone but you.
Absurd, but harmless things, like grown-ups flying kites, are guaranteed to be materially profitless, and so must be valued simply for what they do inside.
So it is with kites and me. They simplify my world for me.

In times like these, it's difficult not to drown in words that won't agree.
It's difficult to know which "expert" to believe. It's difficult to run fast enough to keep up with the change, or hope enough to keep ahead of fear.
Nothing stays the way it was or will remain the way it will become.
Some, trying to find a simple answer, oversimplify: they blame "those others" for what is no one's fault. They grab pat answers and make a mockery of their mentality, which does not change the fact that life's become complex, and we have no easy attic to store our confusions in.
But it is true there must be balance . . . or else insanity.
It takes some source of simplicity to balance our complexity.

So I take some age-old bad advice and make it good for me and go fly a kite.

It's like moving from here to a part of life that makes a sense I understand.

Demands are there, as everywhere—the demand that all parts, wind and kite and me, work together or not at all.

But these demands are clear, and by simple trial and error I find the working balance between hand on string, the length of tail, and the power of the wind.

In it I sort of symbolically reaffirm my own relatedness to the way things are.

In its own silly success I feel that my world and me, which on a string I've left a while, is not really too much, too close, or too complex to bring both kite and mind back down to earth, as everything must eventually.

I have been busy simply flying kites, and found that kites are, for me, part paper and part a kind of prayer.

Not everyone will choose my way, or should.

Not everyone will choose to fly a kite.

But everyone will choose, or should, some word or act of faith.

SUMMER

In March the Spring was little more than Winter's sigh of resignation, that
    no one heard.
We never really knew just when it was it came beyond a Winter-doubt,
    until the Spring was April-old.
But when it came, what April fool, leaning on his rake, would have said
    he'd get enough of Spring or that he'd let it go to weeds?
Yet, somehow, May was overgrown with June.
Somehow, Spring died into Summertime,
And we forgot.

    Almost before we knew what days were doing, Summer covered up the
    Spring.
The frost cracks were filled with selfish moss playing dog-in-the-manger
    to any sign of barrenness.

41

I sometimes think that we were so much taken with Spring's sparse flamboyance that we forgot to keep the grass cut back and knife the plaintain's impertinence off the lawn.
It got ahead of us!
It was Summer and the Spring was gone.

I guess it's futile to imagine that any amount of cutting-back and trimming-up and turning-under could have changed the way it went, even if we had not been greedy to feed our hunger after Wintertime.
You can't keep April underfoot or build a box to hold in May.
I'd almost like to try, because by June there is too much green to see.
The trees get gluttonous for leaves and the lawns for grass.

You'd think I'd be content.
I complained enough last March.
Oh, Summer's good, and Lord knows you can't expect the year to keep its adolescence beyond its time.
It has to go.
It's just that I can't see all that happens in Summer's three-ringed months.

The hollyhocks: they're back, crowding along my fence as if they'd never gone to ground last Fall.
And just because last Winter's birds scattered seeds without my leave—
Though I have to say I could have picked them up or at least pushed them into regimented rows as gardeners are apt to do—
But just for that I've got a crowd of sunflowers, like manic daisies,
Slouching, senseless, and round-shouldered where I never planned for flowers,
And good for nothing, except as boutonnieres for clowns.
At least they hide the peeling paint along the kitchen clapboards where my Spring intentions gone-to-seed left them unscraped.

The grass that was so much to talk about in Spring has grown enough to wet me calf-high, if I dare it to by walking there too early in a day.
So thick it's grown I have to pick a stalk to see its shape.

I might have kept it cut along the edge of things.
I might have, earlier, chased it on hands and knees with clicking shears.
I did put a plank along the path to keep it back.
There wasn't quite enough walking back and forth to clear the path and
    keep it so.
I thought a plank would do, but now the grass is higher than the plank.
The plank won't matter much in time.
The grass will win.
The plank won't.
Winter and Spring and ground will take it bit by bit, and some Summer
    will bury it with green.
Summer is that way about anything bare.

Summer is the year's Puritan that covers Spring's pride with prudery.
A time of green deception that wants to make its modesty retroactive,
    So that it tries to hide even the antique shale that Spring-thaw scattered
    out of hiding where no one cares.
It grows up poplar trees and filigrees of lichens, pads of moss, and toothy
    berry canes in rocks.
It's strange to find a fossil fern in rock and see it being buried now again—
    Summer on Summer: one new and one ten million Summers old.
    And what we didn't clear last Spring: the broken, lost, discarded things
    that April rakes had missed—
What was too far from lawns for us to care about: rusty cans, broken bottles,
    tatters of past picnics—
Pieces of a past—
All gone now under Summer,
    Under clover and under grass,
    Behind grouchy thistles and wild-eyed chicory by roads,
    Beneath milkweed comfortably heavy with pods.
Like the end of time.
Like an August hint of what eternity might be.
Heavy with green and heat and dust to stop whatever noise might dare
    to be,

43

As though nothing had the right to move—
As if to make us think time had stopped and breathing were a blasphemy—
To make a loginess that even blue-spiked heal-all can't cure.
Nothing nervous here but butterflies and poplar leaves.
Late Summer seems like that to me.

A rain may come in Summer with a young, cool, and an unsettling wind
that even the frantic hand-waving of heavy trees can't shush.
A rebel thing that moves against complacency and middle age, and marches
rain across the quiet, like a children's pillow fight before the family's
up.
A show-off yelling thunder upstairs on a hot night when we want a quiet
porch.
The inconsiderate banging of someone making a selfish breakfast before
we want to get so wide awake.
But it can't last.

August is too well set in.
It can't play like adolescents, whose youth defies the lethargy.
It's too old.
We want shade and tall cool times.
Summer is too full of itself in August—self-satisfied.
Summer seems like that, although I know it's not.

There is no time without time!
It's just that leaves can cover up the sight and sound of time.
But in a bush some fledglings hatched, and
I found a soft gray pigeon dead.
I saw these things and they reminded me of time.
A birth.
A death.
This quiet, heavy island in the year is no island without time.
It only seems that way!

My Spring whimsy is only that.
I know I could get too much of Spring.
Who could live with only Spring?
Constant becoming!
Urgency!
Incessant insistence!
We need sometimes a mask to wear so we can't see all we might of birth
    and death;
A clever green grass mask for aromatic air to breathe—if only for a season.
A time to simply be—
We dare not grow too green and self-content.
We dare not go to grass and have no time.

I'm glad September has to come and that I have no choice in it.
I might choose only August, if I could,
    And then have only a season and not a year.
I might, but Fall will come and I'll be glad to have it bring back time,
So I can see this August end,
And know that every day has night, and every night a day.
Each life, but Life itself, must end.
I need to know my own mortality.
Without it neither time nor I have worth,
    Nor the need to try—
    Nor the will to try.

I could not live only in Summer's Great Deception, as I could not live
    in Spring alone.
I need to know of time and feel its passing motion on my face in some
    September wind,
And know that life has time and time is life,
And I, like days and seasons, am passing, being, and yet to be.
Amen.

AUTUMN

August made the Summer seem forever,
And days were only pages routine-torn from kitchen calendars.
Our clocks tick-tocked time, not us.
To us the days were just some more of Summertime.

   Then Autumn came.
It came at night, but left the days for sun and self-deception.
To make us think the Summer stayed.
But Autumn came.
I didn't know it had until I saw cucumber leaves closing limp like used
   yesterdays—one morning after frost.
Cucumbers are better calendars than are calendars.
They know when Summer ends. It's life and death to them.

The first frost seemed out of place: an apprentice ghost practicing its haunting on the shed's east roof where the sun couldn't hide it soon enough even from us.

The first frost mattered little except to gardens.

Whatever had blossomed late was too late now.

As if apologetic for green tomatoes and wilted squash the leaves began to turn: bright bribery trading in old trees for new.

Each frost pushed leaf-green into that nowhere that Summer goes.

Each night uncovered colors that made time more alive than it had been all Summer long.

And it was somehow good that Autumn came.

Clumsy children with rake-handle masts, raking leaf houses in runic rings on lawns;

Noisy carpenters homesteading the yard with rainbow "rooms," content with leaf-beam, leaf-brick, leaf-floor and roof.

An old game no one taught, but children know.

Adults looking as in a looking back from Sunday cars, reluctant to let time pass;

Leaf-lines blurred and soft;

Bronze bushes;

Tailored cattails letting down their hair;

Milkweed seeds like silk spiders walking wind-webs;

Chestnut burrs sharply defiant or, where the drop has broken their spiny spite, pockets spilling round shiny possibilities for pretend pipes, fly cages, and other things that children used to make;

The sumac red as fire in all the brass and brown—a burning bush on some provincial Sinai, if only modern Moses could hear;

Leaves pirouetting in the street;

Stick-tights and burdocks hitching rides to anywhere;

Night frost giving grass previews of Winter snow;

A season like old men bragging of what once was.

A good time . . . and yet . . .

It's hard to let a season go, as Summer went.
It's wistful to gather garden stakes in awkward bundles for wintering;
To watch the Winter come on frost step-by-step,
To count the ladybugs that come inside for warmth.
We live too close to earth to like this ending for all its gold and red.
There is something in all the sound and sight of carnival that has no color.
You sense it in the smell of those first-fallen leaves grown sodden by October,
Or in the musk of morning fog when old warmth and new cold meet—
A vague regret wearing a yellow mask and laughing with a laugh that lacks sincerity.

If I could reshuffle days and weeks like cards, and mark the deck of time to suit myself . . .
Or, like Old Joshua's God could stop the sun at some private Gibeon,
I'd do it, before the rain had knocked the color down.
Failing that, at least I would preserve the trees just as they are, to stand like clowns in Winter's tanbark rings as proof that beauty couldn't die this year.
December would be easier to take like that, if only Fall was "if," not "is."

Once men could cut the field to the last lone stand of grain and make some sense of seasons by plaiting that last swath into a doll—
A corn-maid, a wheat-mother to keep all year in rustic reverence.
But ancient answers hardly do this Fall.
We've long since put away such childish things, and with them our acceptance of first frost and last leaves.
I have no ancient piety!
No corn-maid tends my hearth!
No Yahweh stops my sun and years, and I am grown somehow older late in Fall.
The apple and locust tree try hard to tell a peaceful lie by staying green when maple trees are bare, Winter-ready sticks.

But I've been through a year before, and know that even they will someday
   drop their green pretense and send their leaves to scratch and scrape
   across some January crust of snow.
I shouldn't anticipate it so, not yet, but I can't help this premature regret
   for what will be when gold goes brown in some November mockery
   of Fall.

   So much of what I'd do I can't.
I've grown accepting of the fact.
The very young claim it's growing old.
I say it's growing up.
If not, let them play Joshua and stop the sun.
They'll learn soon enough.
As for me, I'll go with time.

   If we've outgrown the ancient rite of reconciliation, grain gods and such,
And give the Old October Faith empty pumpkin heads instead of prayers,
It's not from lack of love or rituals.
We still have those.
Raking-up is one of them.
It can't be just to clean the lawn no matter what we say, as snow will
   do a better job of that.
I wouldn't say it's only ritual, but there is something ceremonial in it just
   the same.
We go, some night or day, to kick up lawn-leaves to find the rake the
   children left at noon,
To make a pile of tree-ends.
What for?
What use can old leaves be once down and turned to brittle and to brown?
   For jumping piles if young enough?
   To roll laughing in with stem ends poking sharp and tickly bits wriggling
      down jacket necks?
   For adolescent walking through with hand-in-desperate-hand, and scuff
      aside in blind belief that all time is now?

To scatter three feet high by raking harder than we need, as if to tree
   them once again and daub the dark with something bright?
For after-supper children to catch before they touch the ground?
I suppose.
But most of all to be a consolation for adults, who, less convinced than
   younger ones of their own powers to keep things as they are, set a raked-up
   heap on fire and send a low smoke out in gray nostalgia for the nose.
To burn, not out of sheer resentment because they fell, but just to see
   that final color that only fire can show.

   What good are leaves?
   To make an immortality!
   I spread last Autumn's leaves grown Winter-wet and Summer-soft on
      my garden plot.
   Load by load I spread them there and covered them with dirt to rot.
The earth will take them in, and change their shape, and let them come
   again as lettuce leaves and round beet bulbs.
It's a kind of trust I have in what the earth can do—a sense that soil is
   sacred—a faith.
So I make offerings to gods I cannot see and call it "gardening" to give
   it modern shape.
I guess I want to make sure of Spring.

   Once beets and parsnip roots, cool crocks and dill perfume, slatted crates,
      and heaps of corn and hickory nuts were catechisms for the mind.
Once strings of jars on pantry shelves were told like beads.
Once casks and crocks and crates were better things than any cross or
   creed.
Once, but that was once, and we no longer have such harvest hymns laid
   neatly out on staffs of cellar shelves with turnip notes and glass-canned
   lyrics.
For us, the harvest is laid in cellars of ourselves; in row on row of memories.
   No wonder we tend to Autumn crabbiness and hostile window-washing
   and cleaning up.

I've watched women lay out winter coats and boots as though preparing
    suits of armor.
I wonder at this defiant tone we sometimes get in Fall.
Are we so strange to earth as that? So alien to time?
Is Autumn just a colored rag to fling in November's face; an insult to say
    to December 21st?

    Back to the root and to rest.
The trees deserve that much, and so do we!
It's right to go to ground like leaves, if only in the mind.
It's got to be, this sense of ending to prompt a sensed beginning once again.
A lesson in leaves, except for those illiterate with fear, who stop their ears
    with Winter-wool—
A stained-glass story from green to bright to brown and green again.
A simple riddle for those whose year is longer than a year.
For them: an old clean sugar sack to gather Autumn in like shapes of
    chestnuts once-upon-a-time;
For them: a pile of color in the eye for Winter snow, to break its white;
A larder to feed the sometimes discontent.
Remember this short time of life again in February's fireplace fires,
And watch the leaves trudge by as children's mittens and heavy coats.

If there is any sense to seasons it is this:
    That time is timeless and time is Life.
    Not Spring nor Summer, not even Fall is gone.
    Each will be what it becomes, as Winter will be Spring.
The seasons play their walk-on parts, and we can hardly hear the lines,
    much less know all the plot, except the final line:
"Life abides."

BETWEEN TWO SEASONS, A HOLIDAY

From April on, the earth is busy making Summer-shapes from barren soil,
As if it were somehow intent on changing the formless Force of Life
  Into simple shapes where, in Winter, no forms had been that we could
    see.
From April on, the soil makes miracles:
  New grass,
  The first timorous leaves on the village elms,
  The searching tendrils of woodbine that will climb quietly, hand-over-
    hand up whatever will take it closer to the sun.
Even before those last shrunken mounds of snow are gone from the
  shadow-places under the eaves, the earth is busy writing some new
  genesis.

And so it goes from April until the frost sends it back to the root and
the seed for wintering.
So it goes all Summer long.
Miracle after miracle: from seed to sprout to leaf and stalk to its maturity.
Each thing hurrying to be whatever is within itself to be;
Its purpose pushing it up and out:
Rhubarb in a hurry to become broad leaves on sour stems, with nothing
to say it can't, unless we stop it into pie;
Ivy rushing to reach the top, past slower roots of trees, through stones,
determined mindlessly to grow as though the Summer had no end;
Gardens, forgetting they were planned for shelves and dinner plates,
determined to go to seed.
Everything that knows how to grow, busy with becoming, in order that
its kind can come again another year.
From April on, the earth was full of its insistence to cover everything with
green.

But late September frost put an end to this great determination.
The squash leaves folded like used umbrellas;
Tomato leaves and grape wilted, leaving the unripe fruit as proof that
everything that lives must partly fail.
Frost leaves some things unfinished, to be salvaged by human ingenuity
as relish or tomato mince or something else that people know, to make
some failures into a more-or-less success.

Autumn comes in mingled moods, and might not come at all, if we had
anything to say of it.
It seems at times a season of regret, as growing old can seem to those
who see but half the truth.
For all the consolation color is to us:
The maple's oranges and rust,
The elm tree's yellow-gold,
The sumac's red,

We do sometimes regret those last leaves so!

The raucous calls of flocking crows intent on going somewhere else can make it seem as though everything that lives is finished here, and only we must stay behind.

But this is only half the truth!

If most of us were landsmen, instead of what we are,

If our business were with the soil and seasons, as our business used to be,

I half-suspect we'd know the other half-a-truth that Autumn is.

Were that the case, our efforts would be all put up in jars on pantry shelves and bundled into root cellars, instead of being spelled out in charge accounts.

Were that the case, we'd estimate our worth in bins of apples, bags of nuts, and cords of wood laid by for our own wintering—

We'd make January security from cellar rafters hung with hams, from smell of August spices drying in the kitchen up-side-down.

The Summer's paragraph we'd punctuate with potato periods, beet commas, and carrot exclamation marks.

We'd make easier sense of seasons than we'll have to do, if there is any sense to them at all.

These days Thanksgiving is not obvious, as it once was.

There is too much artificial distance between us and earth.

The squash comes packaged.

The turkey too!

Our only effort is to thaw and bake, to tear along the dotted line conveniently.

The paying for it all is antiseptic now, with no smell of earth or human hands to prove these things came from anywhere but some efficient cannery or some neon-lighted marketplace.

Yet, truth is truth.

The earth abides.

Beneath our machined sophistication lies the earth.

Possessions, conveniences, machines and things may cover up the earth's decay and growth, the billboard hide the tree, the endless roads to nowhere cover grass, and human noise grow loud enough that no one hears the wind or cares to watch a sparrow fall.

Yet, even these have come from the earth, and even these return to it one day.

The headlined noise that people make, the momentary and the fad,

The sound of getting, the whimpers of those who have not yet possessed enough,

Easily drown out the almost silent sound time makes when seasons shift;

But seasons flow from Spring to Summer to Fall to that first snow behind our noise.

The shame of it is not the change, but that we will not make a time to touch the earth again and be a part of its incessant miracles.

This time of year seems a between-times time.

Autumn's gone!

The katydids have left no sound, and
There is not heat enough to make them sing again.
Those creatures that go to mud at the first real touch of cold have gone to mud.

But Winter has not quite come.

If we had a sense of seasons we'd make a holiday for solitude,

As our fathers made one of harvest fruits.

Between seasons is a good time to listen to one's own thoughts and make peace with one's environment,

A good time to put aside the getting of too many things,

A time to solve old puzzles we had no time to solve in Summer months.

Now, late Autumn or early Winter or whatever its name may be is a time to see farther than we could when leaves cut off the view.

Now the world reveals itself in more dimensions,
And neither things nor men nor issues can hide in the leafless woods.
We may say it all looks stark and bare, and I suppose it does,
But it also looks clean and clear, for those who dare to look without the
screen of leaves and grass that covered so much before the frost came
on.
A clear view is one thing this time of year allows.
Or if the day turns warm, as days sometimes do this time of year,
We may see that the world is in balance once again.
The year is too.
For every Spring, a Fall.
For every Summer, a Winter's snow.
For every sort of sorrow, I suspect a time to laugh.
For every noise, a silence.

Any Autumn is the sum of its Summer and its Spring.
This year's Spring was late and wet.
The corn was slow, but persistently made a good ensilage crop at last.
Gardens were poor this Summer, but bugs ate about as many weeds as
   vegetables.
Things balance out.
They usually do, if you give them time.

We have to think in longer terms than one season at a time.
There are bad years as well as good.
Bad days too, and good.
Right now things are balanced pretty well . . . right now . . . between
   two seasons . . . between the Winter and the Fall.
Someone said, "To everything, a season. To every purpose, a time."
This time of year it seems that way to me.

Right now, between two seasons, I'd make a holiday of solitude, with that
   clear view the loss of leaves allows, and with a faith that in its time
   my life, like that of earth, is balanced out,
If I have patience enough to see, and if I make a time to touch the earth
   again and see the sense it makes of seasons and of me.

THE FINAL TIME

When I was very young, my yesterdays were few.
Tomorrows came on endlessly and even cold December days were Spring
    to me.
Then a world of timelessness was served at breakfast with my orange juice.
When I was very young and every world was conquerable.

Even now, sometimes, the child in me pretends that nothing ends, especially
    in the Spring.
I am April-fooled by new leaves easily.
This year, when April came and lilacs were just days behind, the crocuses
    kept promises across the lawn, and there was time enough for everything.
Then, behind a bush, I found the feather-fragments and the skull of what
    had once been a bird, and I was not a child again.
I have never been one to know the birds by name.
This one least of all.

This bare beaked bone had never sung to me until I found it there.
And then it sang silently, "Not everything in Spring is yet-to-be."

Some birds die kindlier where children find them and, with hearse-hands
cupped round, bear them off for burial.
No such pitying procession of one had found this bird and made him
Christian by a twig cross on a backyard grave.
Sun and rain, grass and ground, had tried to take him back, but they worked
too slow for me.
A bit of what he was was left to sing, "Not everything is yet-to-be."

Now I am not so very young, and time runs faster than it did.
I am much more mortal than I was at ten.
Day by day my yesterdays pile up and my tomorrows dwindle down.
I know now there is too little time for everything,
And knowing this, today's more precious than all the past that was and
all the might-yet-be can ever be.

Death is not one thing, one time, for everyone, doled out like bargains
one to one.
Too many things and times and places die, for me to be deceived by those
who fear that final time,
For me to think that death comes only in the Wintertime or life in Spring.

For one thing I've seen the cellar holes of houses that used to be on knolls,
their stepstones leading to nowhere now.
In front, old birch;
Along the side the lilacs bow, but not in grief.
They bow with life, as though someone cared they did.
Out back, a gnarled remnant of old orchard climbs the slope bearing nothing
but the proof that someone once loved apple trees, which are left like
old arthritic relatives with nothing left to do.
The barn, in back, a heap of awkward angles, gray beams, and sharp brown
berry canes.

61

I don't know where the people went or when or why,
But places die when people move away.
This falling-down is afterwards and meaningless.

Upstairs where people live is similar.
House attics are full of life that used to be:
Old wallpaper rolls, the records of all the lost ideas of beauty that ever
    marched around the rooms,
An empty fort with all its soldiers gone, now just the fort is left of that
    one Christmas when love came in military dress.
Winters hung up on nails by iceskate strings,
Words, like echoes, in piles of books,
Dolls that only the dust holds now,
Birthdays folded away in partypaper someone meant to use but never did,
The boxed remains of prized possessions, pleasures, plans that we outgrew
    in growing up and going on.
Living is a kind of dying too.

It takes a little while to know how much of life is death and not to dread
    it so.
To sense the equilibrium of the earth,
To be at home in time, and take the limits of both life and love.

Where I grew up was small. Still is.
Yet when I go back, I wonder where the children went.
The ones I see I cannot recognize, except myself.
The other children have vanished into strange adults in a time I somehow
    missed.
Old people greet me still, and will again, but someday that place can go
    to cellar holes and old birch trees for all I care.
You have to learn to let the places go.
At funerals I've watched old men and women look at barren monuments
    as though they had some secret softness that I can't see.

I've watched them walk a visit on the grass, like listening.
The grass is grass to me.
It tells me of today, tomorrow, but nothing more.
I have not lived long enough to know the life in stones or hear the earth
   say how nothing dies that lived.
You must never let the people go.

These are mostly made of small regrets, of love, some pain, a smile or
   two.
If death were only these, memory would be enough to set it right.
If death were but an end to life, I'd know enough to fear it or quietly
   accept the inescapable.
It's the little deaths before the final time I fear.
   The blasé shrug that quietly replaces excited curiosity,
   The cynic-sneer that takes the place of innocence,
   The soft-sweet odor of success that overcomes the sense of sympathy,
   The self-betrayals that rob us of our will to trust,
   The ridicule of vision, the barren blindness to what was once our sense
      of beauty—
These are deaths that come so quietly we do not know when it was we
   died.

The deaths of people are another thing. And not something for public
   scrutiny.
A person's death is a private thing, like grief, like prayer, like birth.
I know nothing of that final time, except what I know of life,
But I know I live and in my life I have so many opportunities to die,
For death is many things and times,
Before the days are gone,
But I have, yet, a while, and things to be, and much to do.

Text design and illustration: David Dawson
Cover design: Bruce Jones
Type: 11pt. Palatino leaded 2 pts
Typesetter: Gulbenk Typesetting